ARTS & CRAFTS PRIMARY 3

Jane Martin

Art consultant:
Lissete Madrazo

Course consultant:
Harriet Thompson

BY ME

My name is:

....

....

....

Contents

0 What is Art?

Art is all around us.
There are many different forms of Art.

1 Match.

photograph b   mosaic ☐   collage ☐   building ☐   painting ☐   sculpture ☐

a *Lizard,* Antoni Gaudí. 1900-1914

b Photo by José B. Ruiz

c *Tenerife Auditorium,* Santiago Calatrava. 2003

d *Meditative Rose,* Salvador Dalí. 1926

e *The Caress of a Bird,* Joan Miró. 1967

f *Man with a Moustache,* Pablo Ruiz Picasso. 1914

2 Can you think of other examples of Art?

Artists draw ideas in a sketchbook. First, plan a cover for your sketchbook. Then, make a sketchbook to draw your ideas.

1. Fold the paper in half.

2. Staple the pages together.

3. Decorate the cover.

My sketchbook design

Finished? Draw something in your sketchbook.

1 Self-portraits

The Frame, Frida Kahlo. 1938

(1) How is the woman in the painting similar to the woman in the photo?

(2) How do artists create portraits?

This is a self-portrait. It's a painting of the artist by the artist.

There are more than fifty self-portraits by Frida Kahlo.

Many artists paint self-portraits. First, they look carefully at their face. Then, they show the shape, size and position of the different parts of their face.

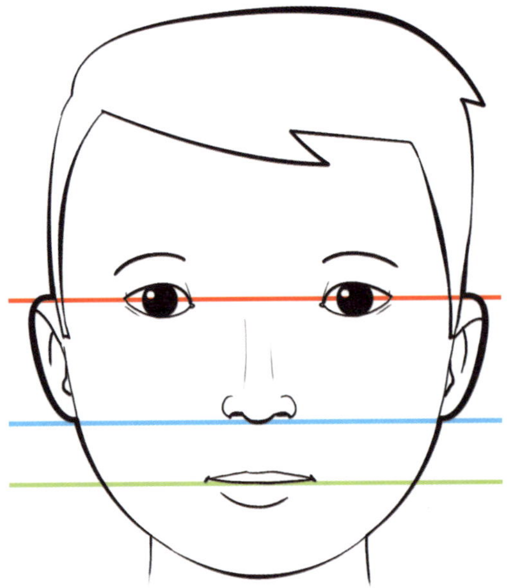

Does this artist show the shape, size and position of the parts of her face?

2 Activity 1 3 Activity 2

3 Complete the portraits.

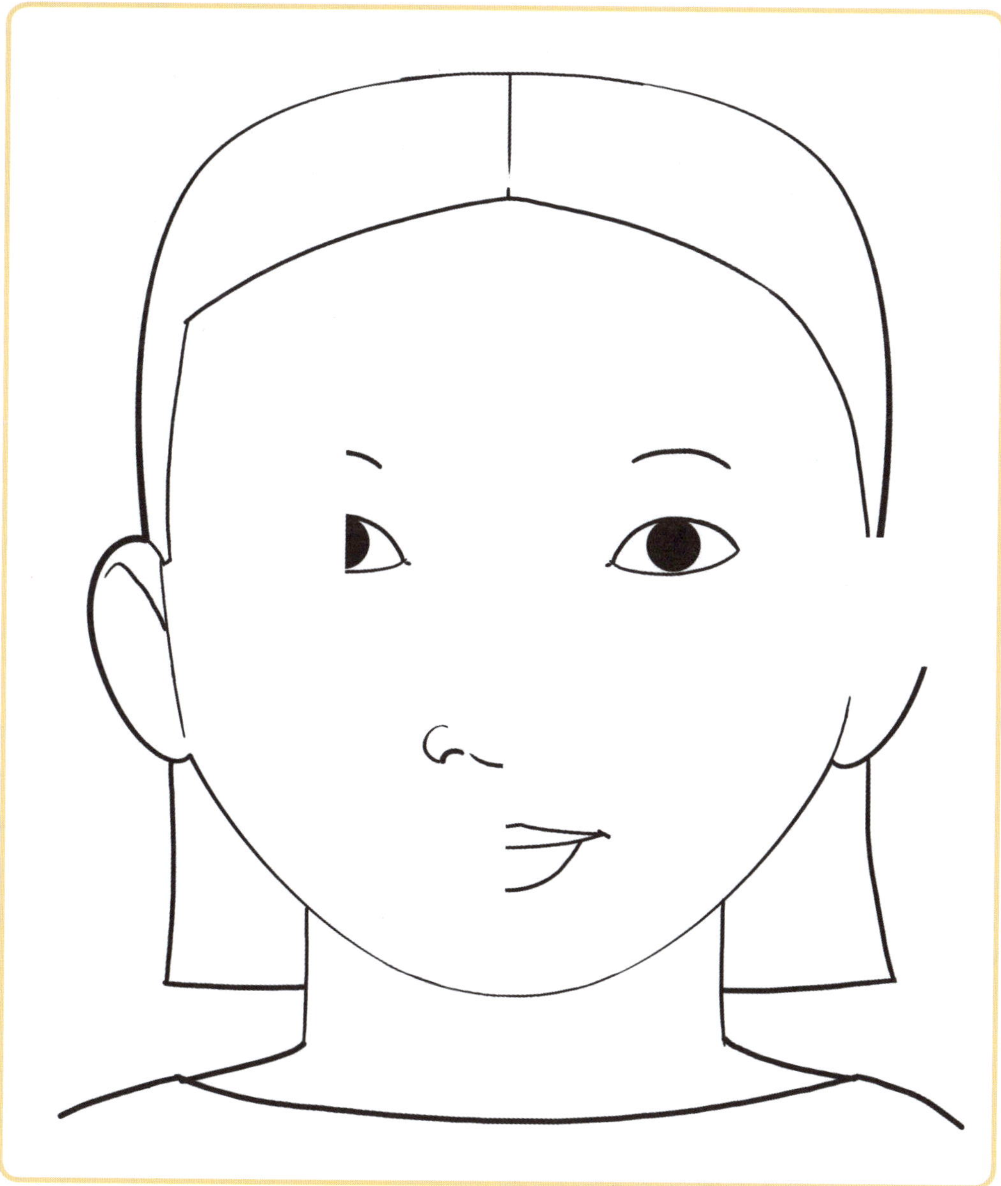

Finished?
Colour the portraits.

Portraits

Artists use lines to divide the head.
Then, they draw the parts of the face.

1 Draw eyes on the red line.

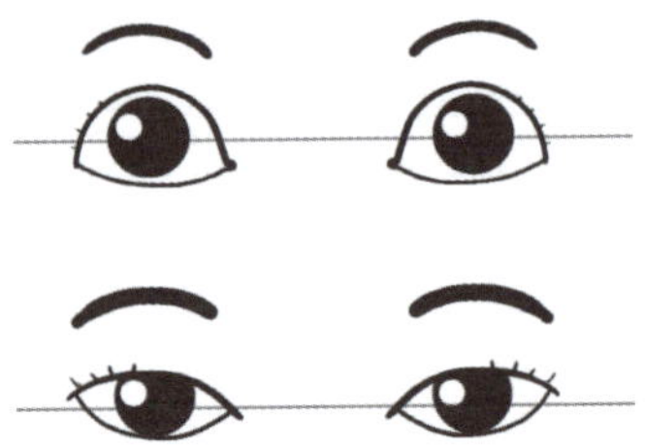

2 Draw a nose above the blue line.

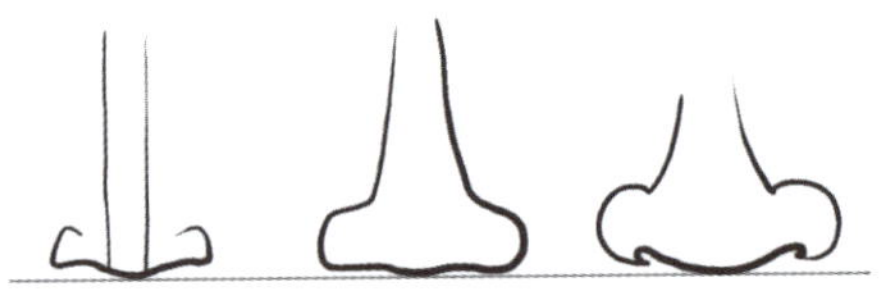

3 Draw a mouth on the green line.

4 Draw hair. Colour.

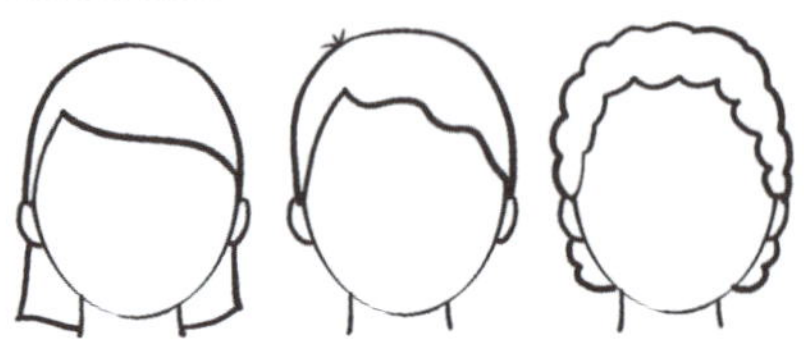

Finished? Draw a portrait of a friend.

My self-portrait

You can draw a self-portrait. Look in a mirror. Look carefully at the shape, size and position of the parts of your face.

Step 1

Draw your head.
Add your neck and shoulders.

Step 2

Draw your eyes in the centre.
Add eyebrows.

Step 3

Draw your nose,
mouth and ears.

Step 4

Draw your hair.
Colour.

Finished? Draw your favourite things around your portrait.

2 Still life

Guitar on a Table, Juan Gris. 1916

① What colours can you see in this painting?

② How do artists use colour in a still life?

This is a still life. It's a painting that shows non-living things.

Artists mix a primary colour with a secondary colour to make a new colour.

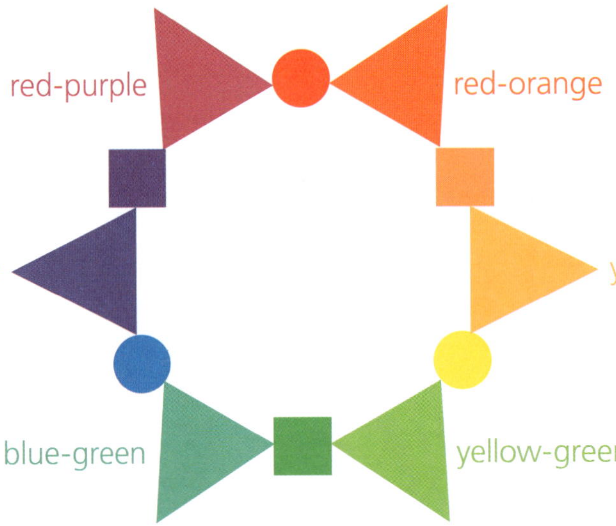

Can you find the colour red-purple in this still life painting?

4 Activity 1 5 Activity 2

3 Mix the primary and secondary colours to make a new colour. Match the colour of the objects.

Finished? Draw an object you can see. Mix colours.

My still life

Artists carefully **observe** objects to draw a still life.

1. Help your teacher choose objects.

2. Observe and draw the objects.

3. Colour.

Finished? Draw a window. What's outside?

My Gris guitar

There is a guitar in Juan Gris's painting. You can make a guitar. Just add colours, strings and play.

Step 1

Cut the paper roll.

Step 2

Mix colours.

Step 3

Glue the paper roll to the tray.

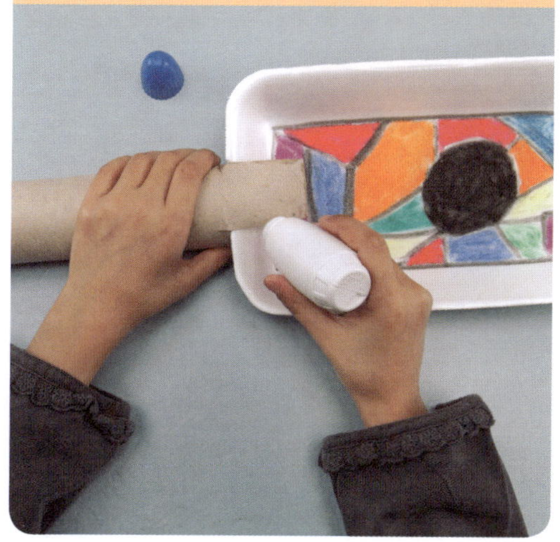

Step 4

Add elastic bands.

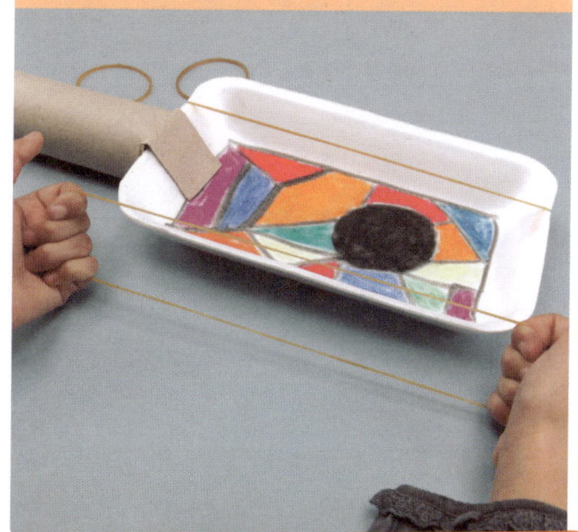

Finished? Add more colours to the outside of your guitar.

3 Collages

Icarus, Henri Matisse. 1947

① What do you think this person is doing?

② How do artists make collages?

Artists can cut and stick paper to make a **collage**.

This collage shows a person. The person is the **positive shape**. The space around the positive shape is the **negative shape**.

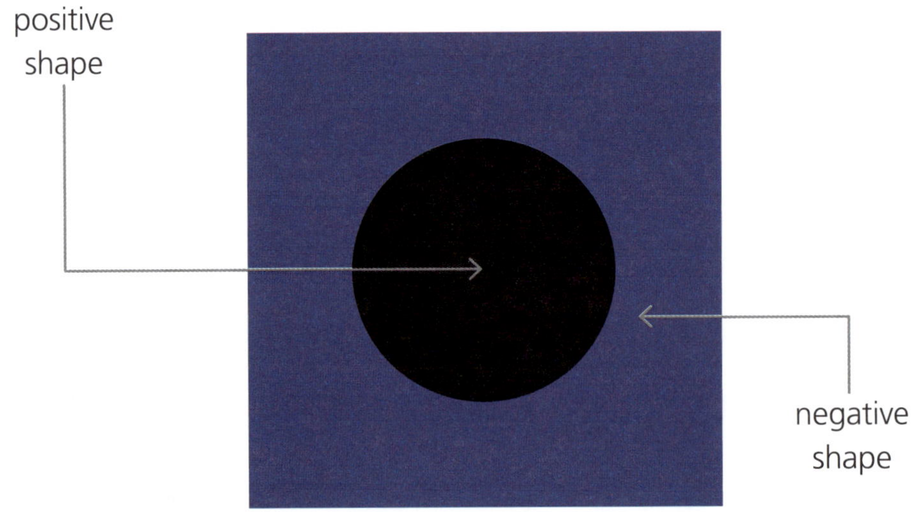

Can you see other positive shapes in this collage?

⁶ Activity 1 ⁷ Activity 2

3 Choose a positive shape. Add details and colour.

Finished? Colour the negative shape one colour.

Let's move

Artists draw lines and shapes to show a figure in motion.

1 Use lines to draw a figure in motion.

2 Add circles for the neck, stomach and joints.

3 Draw the shape of the body. Colour.

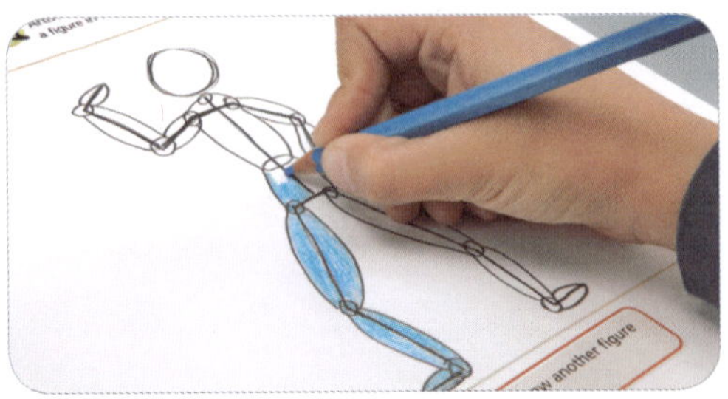

Finished? Draw another figure in motion.

My collage

You can make a collage that shows motion with positive and negative shapes.

Step 1

Draw a body in motion.

Step 2

Cut out the body.

Step 3

Glue it on coloured paper.

Step 4

Glue the negative shape.

Finished? Draw the outlines of objects in your classroom.

REVIEW 1 Art in nature

Mandrill, John Gerrard Keulemans. 1907

1 Does this animal look real? Why or why not?

2 How do artists show animals?

Many artists observe animals in nature.

They observe the **shape**, **size** and **position** of animals' body parts. They also observe animal **coverings**.

Animals have got different coverings.

Animals have got smooth skin, fur, feathers, scales or a shell.

What animal coverings can you see in this painting?

8 Activity 1 9 Activity 2

Animal coverings

Artists use texture to show animal coverings.

Step 1

Draw the outline of an animal.

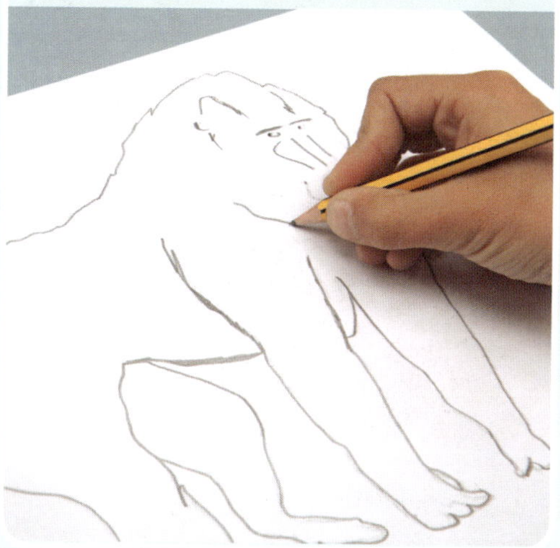

Step 2

Paint with one colour.

Step 3

Paint lines and shapes with different colours.

Step 4

Use objects to create texture.

Finished? Make texture rubbings with objects in your classroom.

My animal poster

We need to protect animals and their habitats.
Artists make posters to help protect animals.
You can make an animal poster, too.

Next step: Work together to make a poster.

Step 5

Use felt tips to draw details.

Step 6

Glue materials on to your animal.

Step 7

Cut out.

Finished? Plan your poster. What do you want to say?

Our animal presentation

1. Make an animal poster.
2. Create a title for your poster.
3. Talk about your poster.

- How did you make your poster?
- Is it a mammal, bird, fish, reptile or amphibian?
- Is it a carnivore, herbivore or omnivore?
- What covering does it have?
- What is its habitat?
- Is it in danger of extinction?
- How can we help protect this animal?

4 Mosaics

Mosaic, The Alhambra Palace. AD 1300

1 What shapes can you see in this mosaic?

2 How do artists make mosaics?

Artists make mosaics with small **pieces** of different materials. They put the pieces together like a **puzzle**.

The Alhambra Palace in Granada has got lots of tile mosaics on the **walls** and **floor**.

These mosaics are made up of geometric **patterns**.

Can you find patterns in this mosaic?

11 Activity 1 12 Activity 2

3 Colour the patterns in the mosaic.

Finished? Draw a pattern with flowers.

Making patterns

Artists repeat lines, shapes and colours to make patterns in a mosaic.

1. Continue the first two patterns.

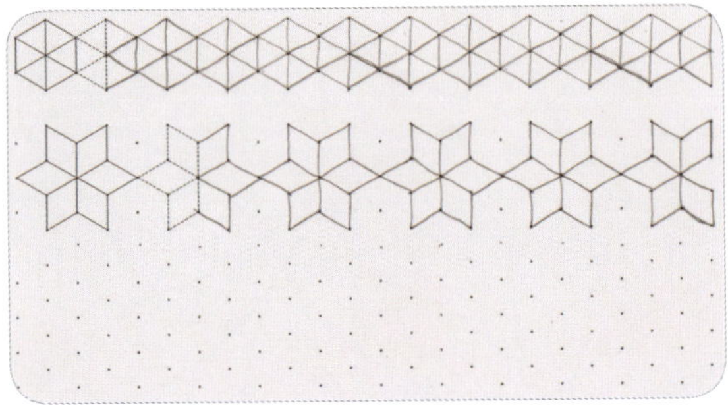

2. Add a new pattern.

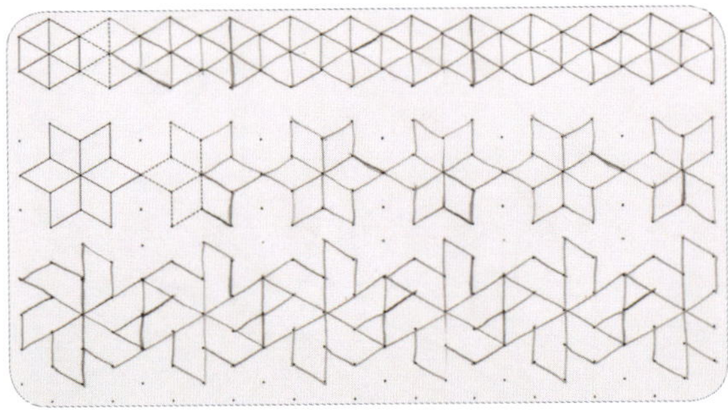

3. Colour all the patterns.

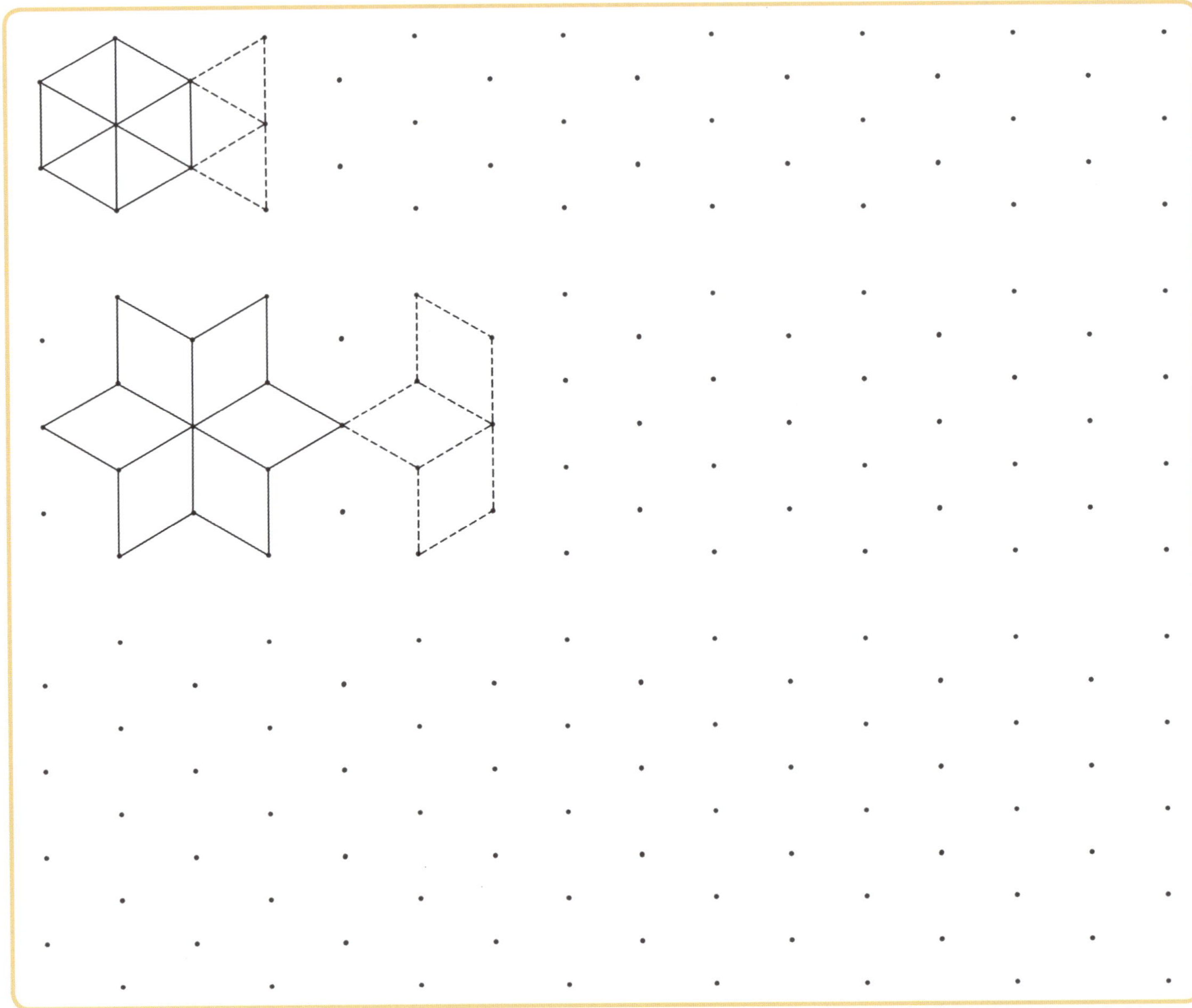

Finished? Make more geometric patterns.

My mosaic flower

You can make a mosaic flower with geometric shapes.
Make a pattern that goes around and around.
Then, make a mosaic garden with friends.

Step 1

Colour the shapes.

Step 2

Cut out the shapes.

Step 3

Make a flower pattern.

Step 4

Glue.

Finished? Draw a picture of your mosaic flower.

Template page 65

5 Near and far

Tropical Forest with Monkeys, Henri Rousseau. 1910

① How many animals can you see in this painting?

② How do artists show objects near and far?

Objects in the foreground look nearer than objects in the middle ground and background.

Artists make objects in the background smaller so that they look further away.

Why is the monkey in the background the smallest monkey in the painting?

13 Activity 1 14 Activity 2

3 Cut and glue the trees and monkeys in the **background**, **middle ground** and **foreground**. Colour.

Finished? Draw, cut and glue more animals and plants in your jungle habitat.

Template **page 67**

The desert

Artists can draw objects big or small.
They can show objects that look near or far away.

1. Draw a cactus in the background.

2. Draw a cactus in the middle ground.

3. Draw a cactus with a lizard in the foreground.

Finished? Add more desert animals to your habitat.

My habitat

Artists can show different habitats with plants and animals. You can make a habitat with plants and animals in the foreground, middle ground and background.

Step 1

Cut and fold the template.

Step 2

Cut and glue the plants in the background. Add an animal.

Step 3

Cut and glue another animal in the middle ground.

Step 4

Cut, fold and glue the foreground.

Finished? Add details in your foreground, middle ground and background.

Template page 69

6 Kites

① Which is your favourite kite?

② How are kites different?

The **kite** was invented more than two thousand years ago. Artists make many different types of kites.

Some kites are flat. Other kites are made up of **forms**. Forms have got three **dimensions**: **height**, **width** and **depth**.

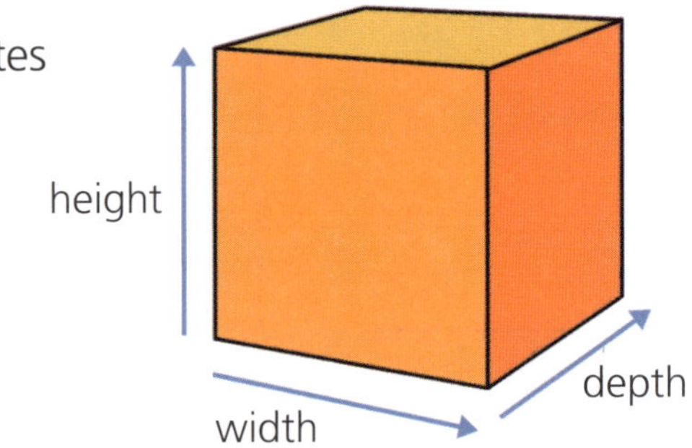

Geometric forms:

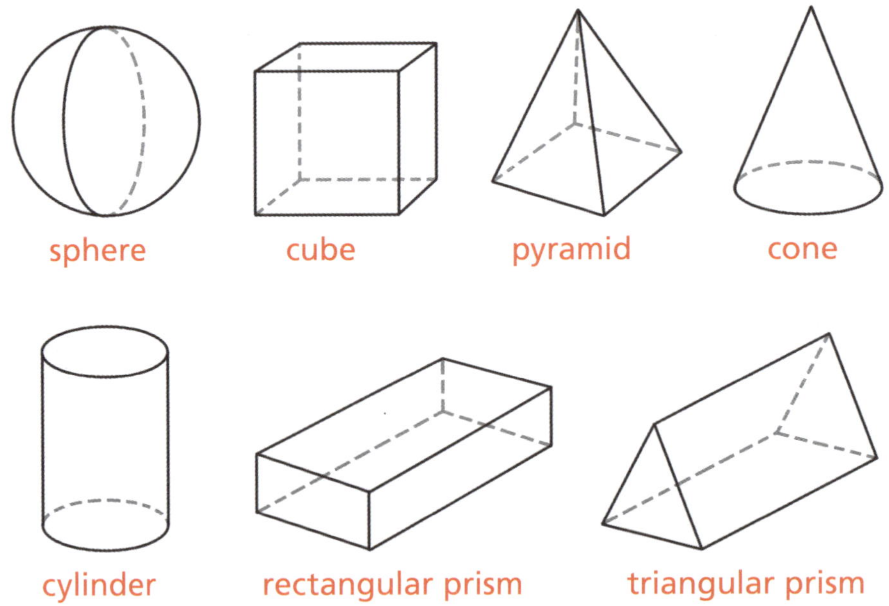

Which kite is made up of geometric forms?

15 Activity 1 16 Activity 2

3 Draw lines from the shapes to the point. Colour the forms.

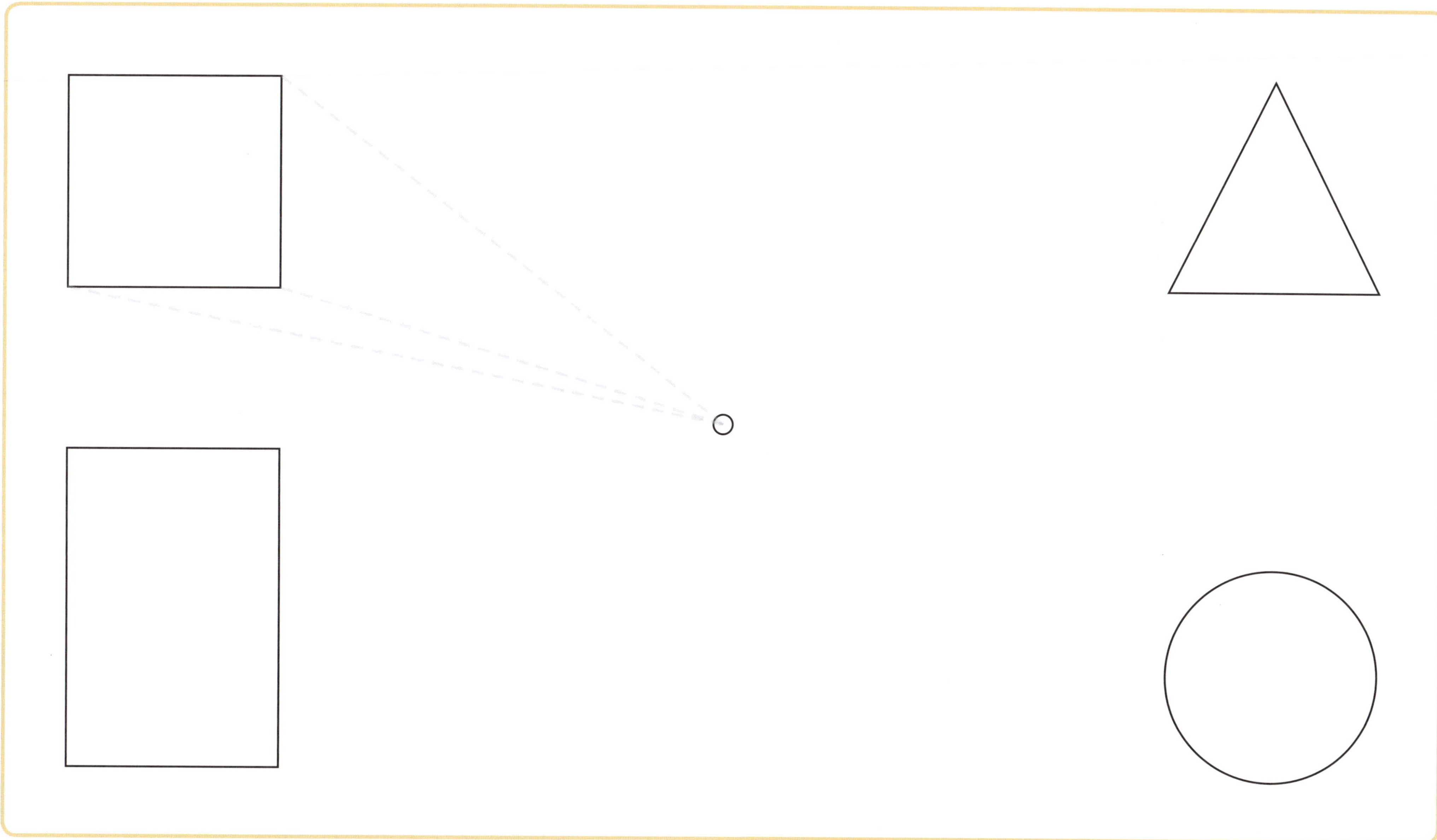

Finished? Add more shapes and draw lines to the point.

3-D forms

Artists can use different materials to construct forms.

1. Identify and draw the four forms that are made up of straight lines only.

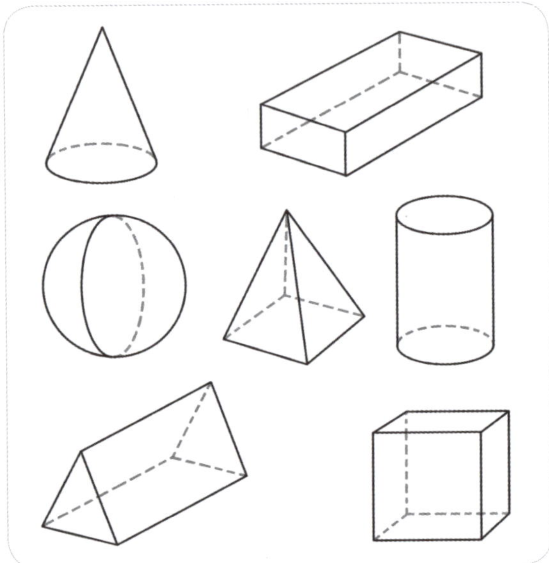

2. Use plasticine and toothpicks to construct a form.

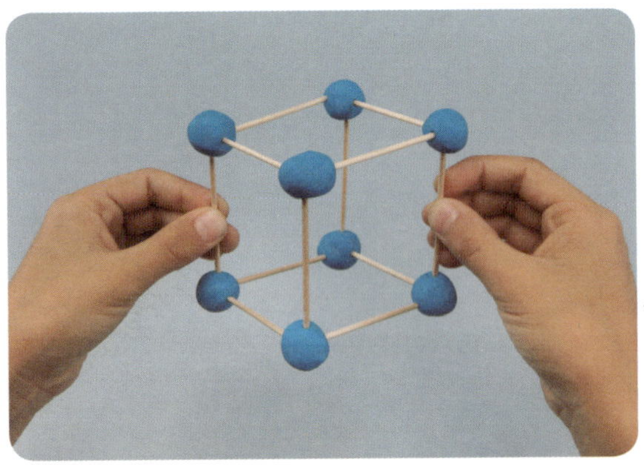

1	2
3	4

Finished? Construct more forms.

My kite

Kites are popular all over the world. Families in Japan celebrate Children's Day and decorate their houses with carp kites.

Step 1

Colour the carp. Cut.

Step 2

Glue.

Step 3

Glue the tail.

Step 4

Add a string around the mouth.

Finished?
Design a new kite.

Template page 71

REVIEW 2 Landscapes

Stone City Iowa, Grant Wood. 1930

1 Would you like to live here? Why or why not?

2 How can artists show forms in landscapes?

Landscapes are made up of three main parts:

a foreground,

a middle ground

and a background.

This artist shows patterns and forms in the landscape.

Some forms look near and some forms look far away.

What can you see in the foreground, middle ground and background of this landscape?

17 Activity 1 18 Activity 2

Plan a landscape

Landscapes can show different natural features, such as mountains, hills or the beach.

Step 1

Plan a landscape.
Add a background.

Step 2

Add a middle ground.

Step 3

Add a foreground.

Finished? Add pictures of natural and man-made features to your landscape.

Forms and patterns

Artists can show many different forms and patterns in a landscape.

Next step: Work together to make a big landscape.

Step 4

Make natural and man-made features.

Step 5

Glue the features on the landscape.

Step 6

Add more materials to make patterns.

Finished? Draw a picture of your landscape.

Our landscape presentation

1. Build a big landscape.
2. Talk about your artwork.

- How did you make your landscape?
- What is in the foreground, middle ground and background?
- What natural features are in your landscape?
- What man-made features are in your landscape?
- What plants and animals are in your landscape?
- How can we take care of natural landscapes?

7 Land art

Artwork by Julia Brooklyn and Richard Shilling

① Which natural materials can you see in this land art?

② How do artists make land art?

Artists create land art with natural materials, such as soil, rocks, and parts of plants.

Artists put these materials together to make sculptures with organic lines, shapes and forms.

Most land art is completed outside. The artist can take a photo of the land art and share it with other people.

What does this land art show?

20 Activity 1 21 Activity 2

3 Cut out photos of organic shapes and forms. Glue them on the sand to make land art.

Finished? Draw different organic lines, shapes and forms from nature.

Nature prints

Artists can use natural materials to make **stamps**. They add paint to transfer the image to make a nature **print**.

1. Add paint.

2. Print.

3. Repeat with other materials.

Finished? Share your stamps with your classmates.
Make another nature print.

My rock animal

Rocks have got many different shapes and sizes.
We can use rocks to make Art.
Choose a rock and look at its shape and size.
How can you make your rock look like an animal?

Step 1

Choose a rock.
Think of an animal.

Step 2

Paint your rock.

Step 3

Plan the details
of your animal.

Step 4

Paint the details.

Finished? Draw a picture of your rock animal and record facts about this animal.

8 Inventions

Aerial Screw, Leonardo Da Vinci. 1493

Flying Machines, Leonardo Da Vinci. 1490

1. Can you identify these forms of transport?

2. Where do artists get ideas for new inventions?

Leonardo Da Vinci is a very famous artist. He was also a **musician**, **scientist** and **inventor**, who got his ideas by observing nature.

Da Vinci used his sketchbooks to draw ideas for **flying machines** many years before these machines were invented.

Which idea for a flying machine do you think was inspired by a seed?

22 Activity 1 23 Activity 2

3 Complete the objects. Colour.

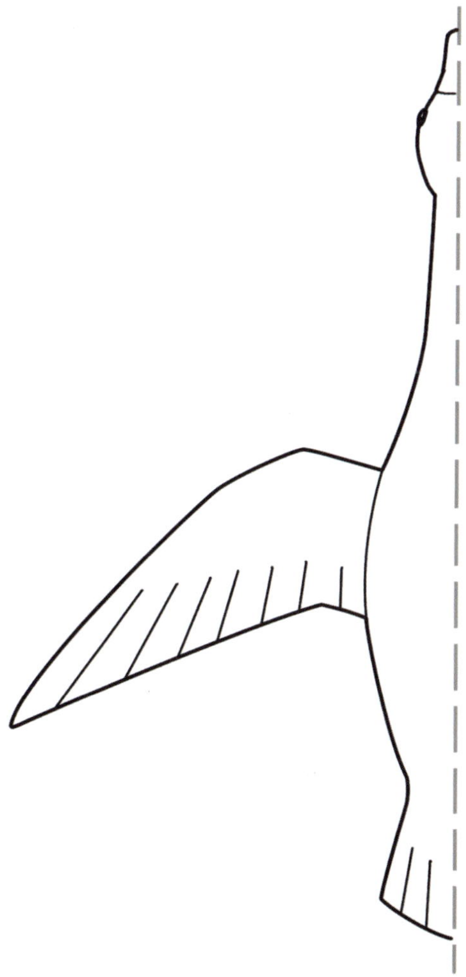

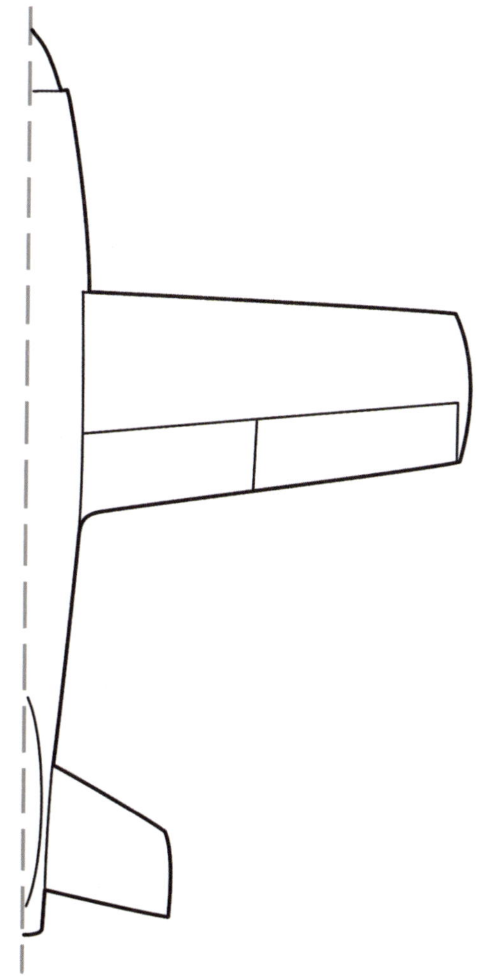

Finished? Draw a picture of the sky filled with animals and objects that fly.

Be an inventor

Leonardo Da Vinci observed nature and used his imagination to draw inventions.

1. Look at pictures of animals and objects that fly.
2. Invent a new flying machine.

3. Colour.

Finished? Invent a new form of transport.

Paper plane

People still observe and imitate nature to design modern planes.

Step 1

Fold the paper.

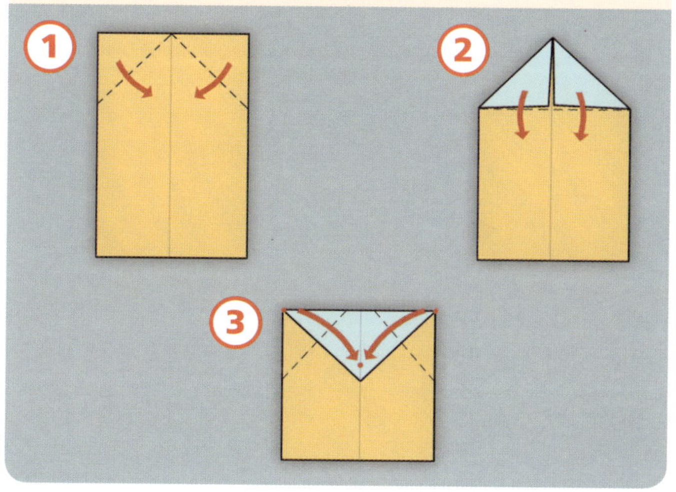

Step 2

Fold the wings.

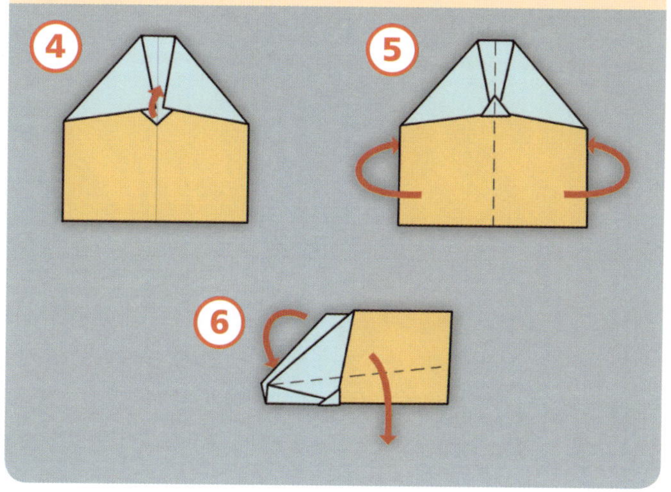

Step 3

Colour.

Finished?
Fly your plane.

9 Illustration

Illustration by Nacho Gómez. 2012

① Where can you see movement in this illustration?

② What do illustrators do?

Illustrators draw pictures to tell stories. These pictures are called illustrations.

Illustrators draw pictures of the characters in a story.

The lines in illustrations show movement.

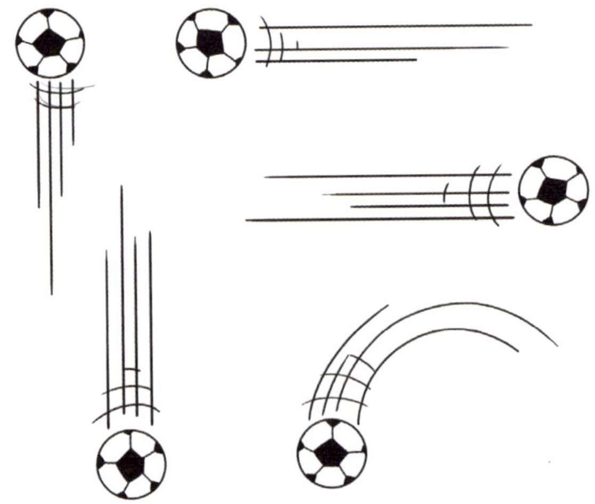

Movement goes forwards and backwards, side to side, up and down, and around and around.

Do you think the girl scores a goal?

24 Activity 1 25 Activity 2

3 Draw lines to show movement. Colour.

Finished? Draw a picture of yourself doing your favourite activity. Draw lines to show movement.

Create a character

Stories have different characters.
Illustrators show us what a character looks like.
They also show us the personality of the character.

1. Read the questions:

- Is your character a person, an animal or a monster?
- How old is your character?
- What does your character look like?
- What does your character wear?

2. Draw your character.

Finished? What does your character like to do? Draw.

Comic strip

Some illustrators create comic strips. A comic strip is a sequence of drawings that tells a story.
You can use your character to create a comic strip.

Step 1

Read the sentence and draw your character.

Step 2

Read the other sentences and draw more pictures.

Step 3

Draw what's in the box.

Step 4

Add lines to show movement. Colour.

Finished? Draw a new comic strip with your character.

Template page 73

REVIEW 3 Buildings

Guggenheim Museum Bilbao, Frank Gehry. 1997

1 What do you think this building is used for?

2 How do artists design buildings?

Artists design new buildings for villages, towns and cities. These artists are called architects.

Architects think about who the building is for and what the building is used for. They also use their imagination and create new designs.

First, architects make plans for a building. Then, they make a model of the building.

Why do you think architects make a model?

26 Activity 1 27 Activity 2

My model building

Architects get inspiration from the world around them. They think of new ways to design new buildings.

Step 1

Choose materials for your model.

Step 2

Glue.

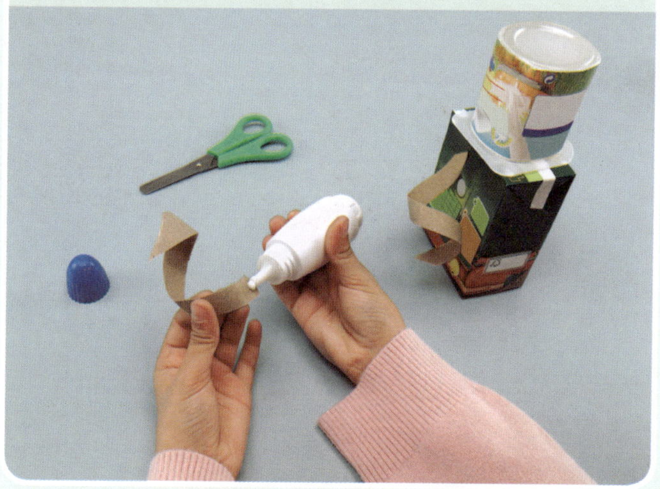

Step 3

Paint.

Finished? Draw a picture of your building. Plan the windows, doors and other details.

My building in the city

What lines, shapes, colours, patterns, textures and forms can architects use to design new buildings?

Next step: Work together to make a city.

Step 4

Add details to your buildings.

Step 5

Add a sign.

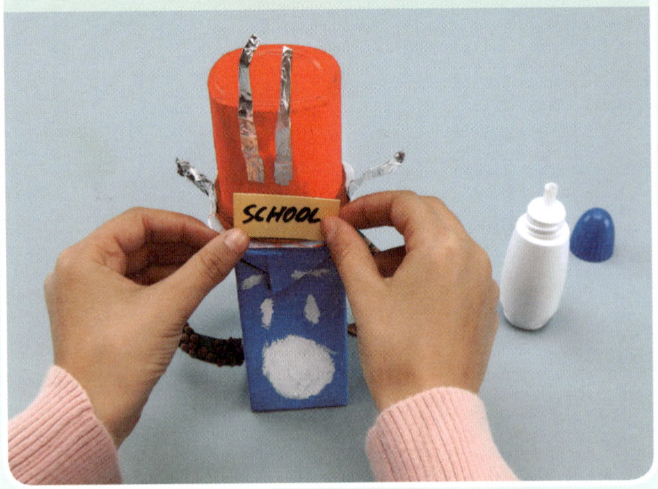

Step 6

Make roads for your city and add your buildings.

Finished? Colour the roads and the area around your building.

Our city presentation

1 Make a city.

2 Talk about your artwork.

- How did you make your model?
- What does your city look like? Describe it.
- What is the building used for?
- Who will use your building?
- Why is your building important?

Halloween house

People celebrate Halloween in different ways. Children go trick-or-treating and go to parties. They listen to stories and watch films with scary characters.

bat

black cat

ghost

monster

mummy

spider

witch

Step 1

Cut out the house.
Open windows and doors.

Step 2

Glue onto coloured paper.

Step 3

Draw and colour.

Step 4

Decorate.

Template **page 75**

Winter snowflake

Snowflakes fall from the sky in many different shapes and sizes. All snowflakes have a shape with six sides, but each snowflake is unique.

Step 1

Make a circle. Cut it out.

Step 2

Fold into six parts.

Step 3

Cut shapes.

Step 4

Open your snowflake.

Christmas tree

People celebrate Christmas in many different ways. They sing carols and give presents. They decorate their homes with lights, tinsel, holly and a Christmas tree.

People also send Christmas cards to say *Happy Christmas!* to family and friends.

Step 1

Fold and cut the red paper. Fold the green paper.

Step 2

Fold the red paper again. Draw and cut out a tree.

Step 3

Cut the trees in half.

Step 4

Glue the trees onto the green paper. Decorate.

Peace Day

People in the world speak different languages and have different beliefs.

On Peace Day we think about world peace and how we can all live together and respect each other.

Step 1

Colour a different pattern in each puzzle piece.

Step 2

Cut out.

Step 3

Give a puzzle piece to your partner.

Template page 77

Easter egg

Some people celebrate Easter with **Easter eggs**. In spring, new plants grow and animals are born. Paint an Easter egg and celebrate spring!

Step 1

Decorate the Easter egg with crayons.

Step 2

Paint.

Step 3

Cut out.

Template **page 79**

Friendship Day

Friends are important. Friends play with you, talk to you, listen to you and help you. Say thank you to your friends on Friendship Day and give them a friendship bracelet.

Step 1

Tie a knot with three strings of wool.

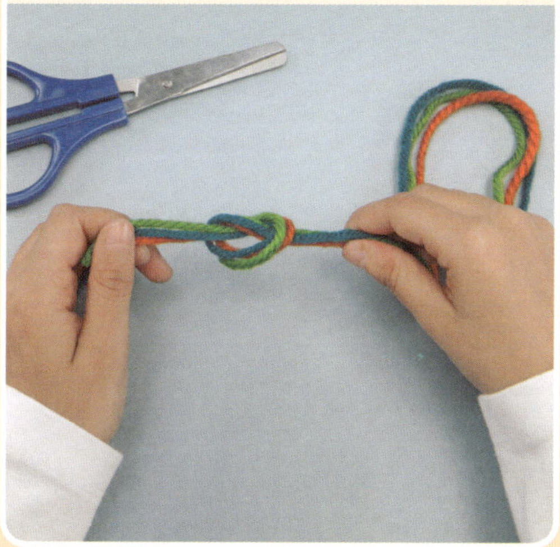

Step 2

Pull the green string over the red string.

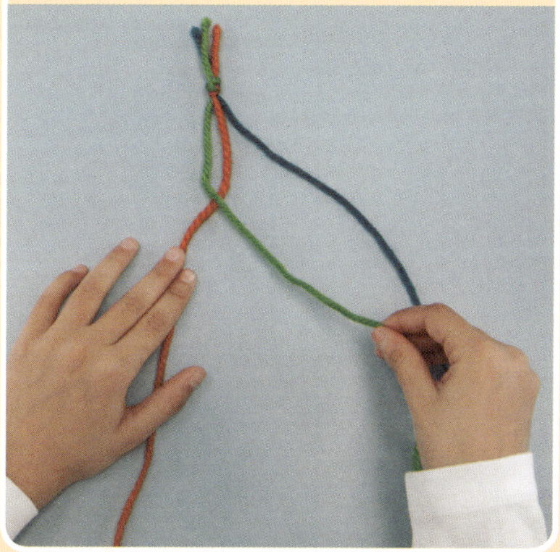

Step 3

Pull the blue string over the green string.

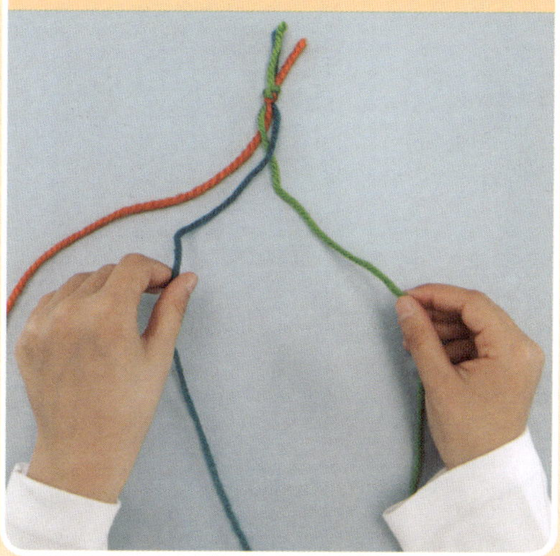

Step 4

Repeat.
Tie a knot.

How can you describe the artwork?

It's a/an...

collage

illustration

mosaic

landscape

self-portrait

still life

I can see a/an...

It's got...

There is / There are...

What's your opinion of the artwork?

I like the...

lines

shapes

patterns

colours

textures

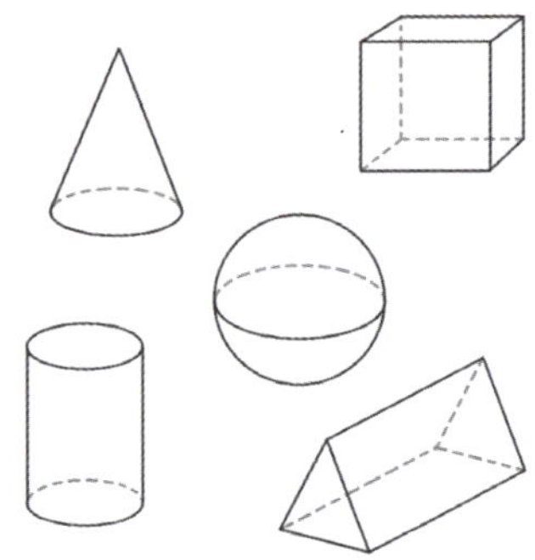

forms

space

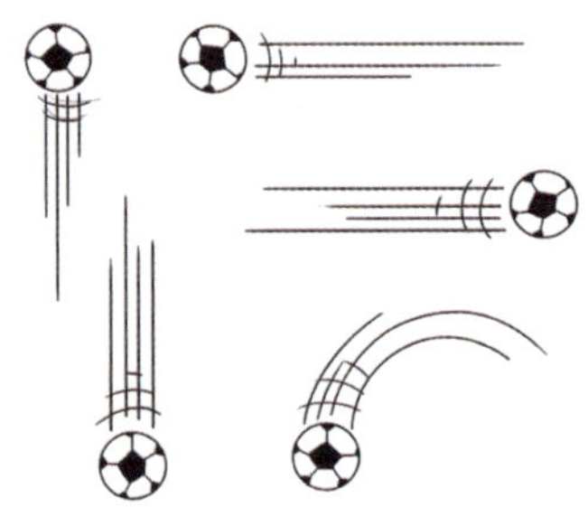

movement

materials

Art materials

Paper

card

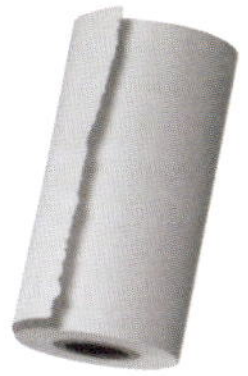
continuous paper

paper

tissue paper

Glue

glue stick

white glue

Mould

clay

plasticine

Cut

scissors

Draw and colour

coloured pencils

crayons

felt tips

oil pastels

pencil

Paint

paintbrush

poster paint

water

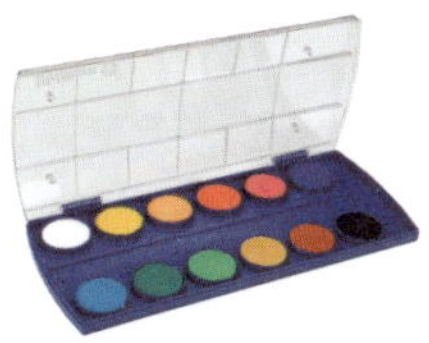
watercolours

Extra materials

elastic bands

glitter

leaf

lentils

mirror

paper roll

pencil sharpener

recycled materials

rock

rubber

ruler

string

tape

toothpicks

tray

wool

Colour with coloured pencils and crayons

Colour inside the lines.

Colour with felt tips

Press softly.

Colour with oil pastels

Mix colours. Blend colours.

Cut

Cut along the lines carefully and slowly.

Glue

Put glue in the centre and on the edges.

Mould

Gently change its shape with your fingers.

Paint

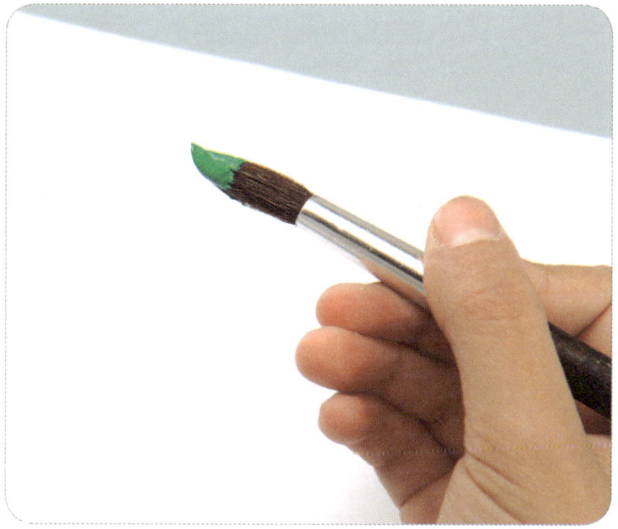

Put paint on the tip of the paintbrush.

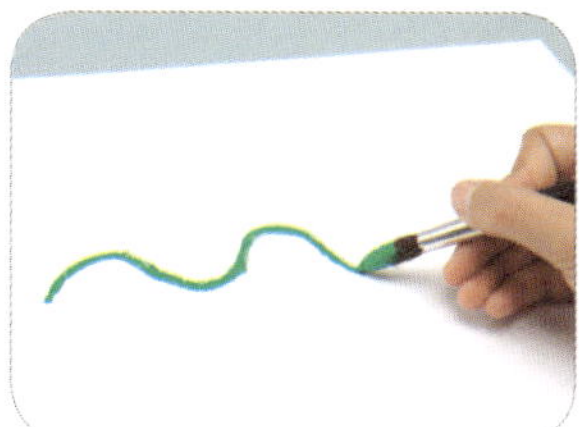

Paint with the tip for thin lines.

Push down for thick lines.

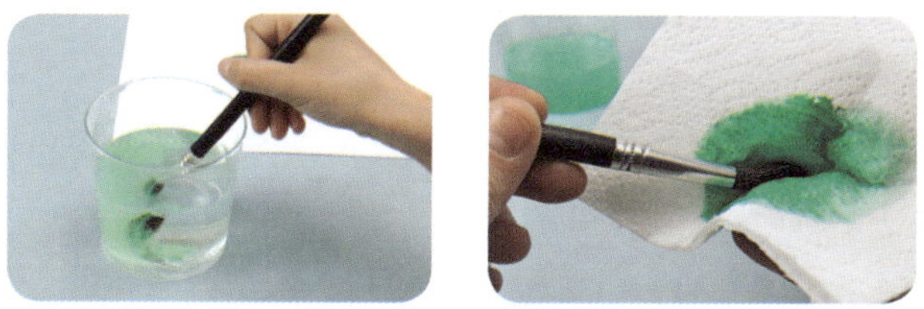

Clean and dry your paintbrush.

Print

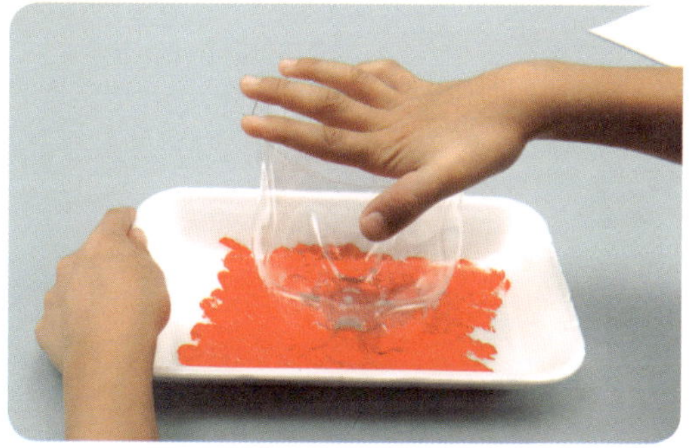

Dip an object in the paint.

Press down on a piece of paper.

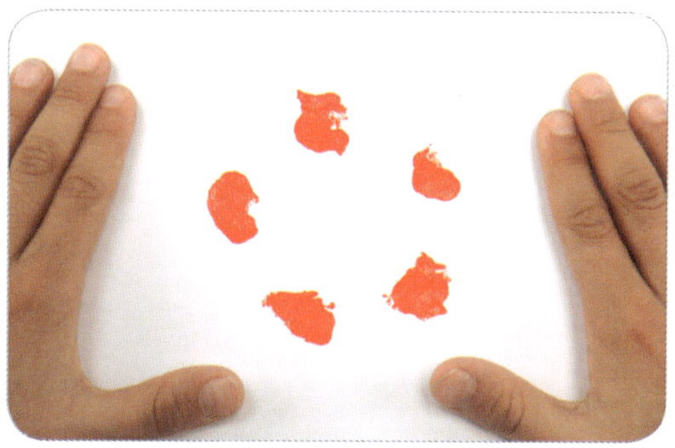

Carefully lift the object.

Work together

Share your ideas.

Plan your project.

Take turns.

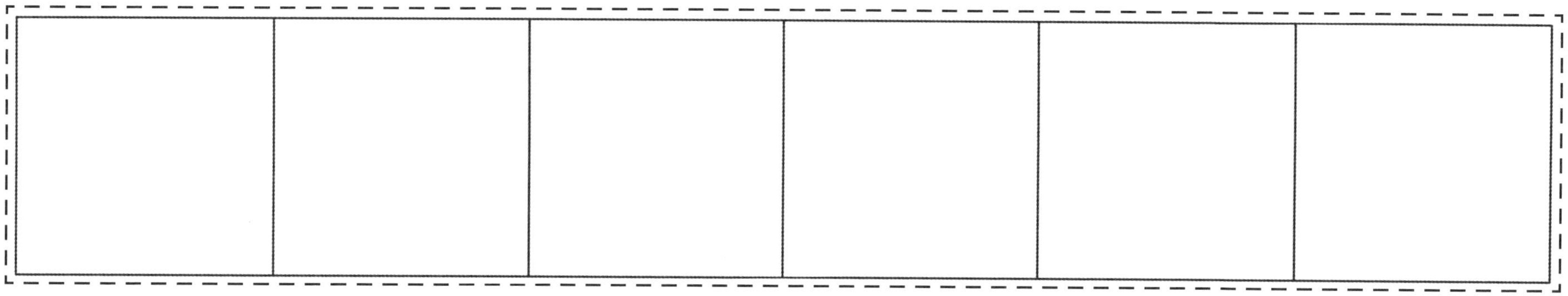
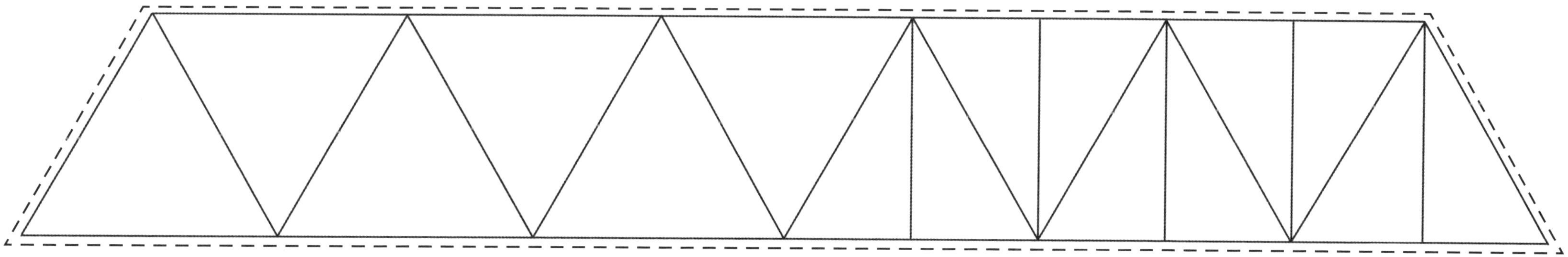
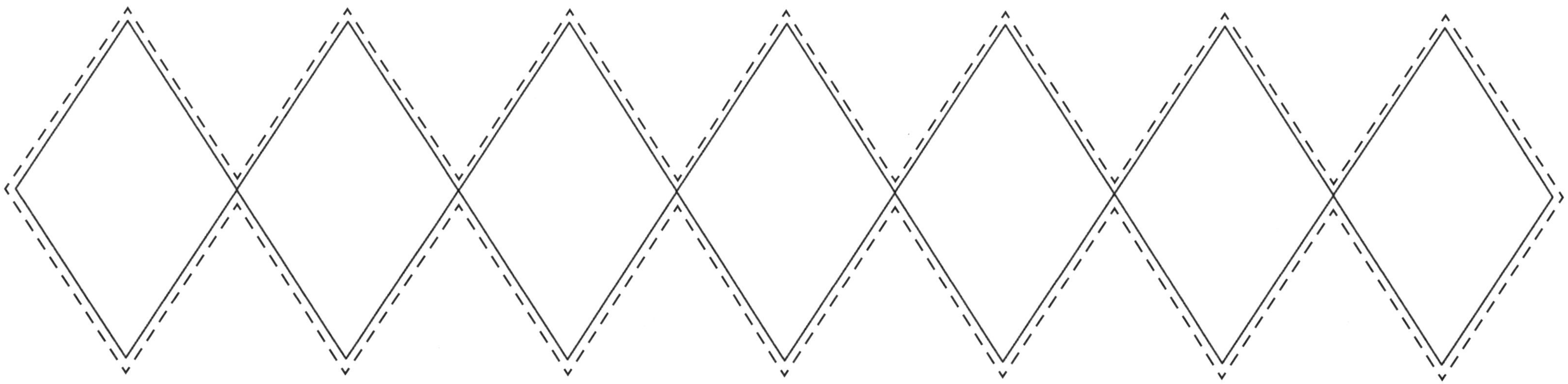

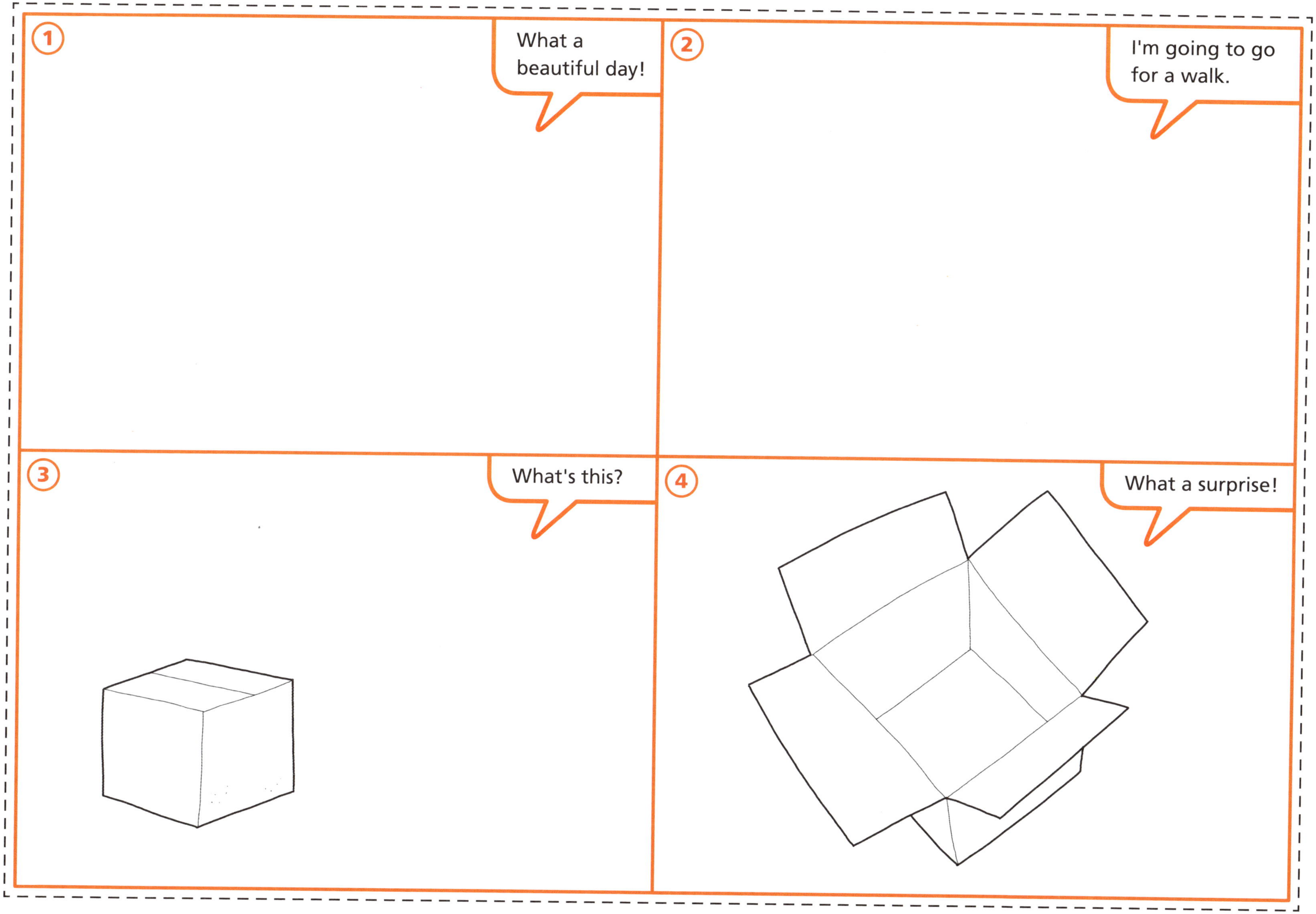
1
What a beautiful day!
2
I'm going to go for a walk.
3
What's this?
4
What a surprise!

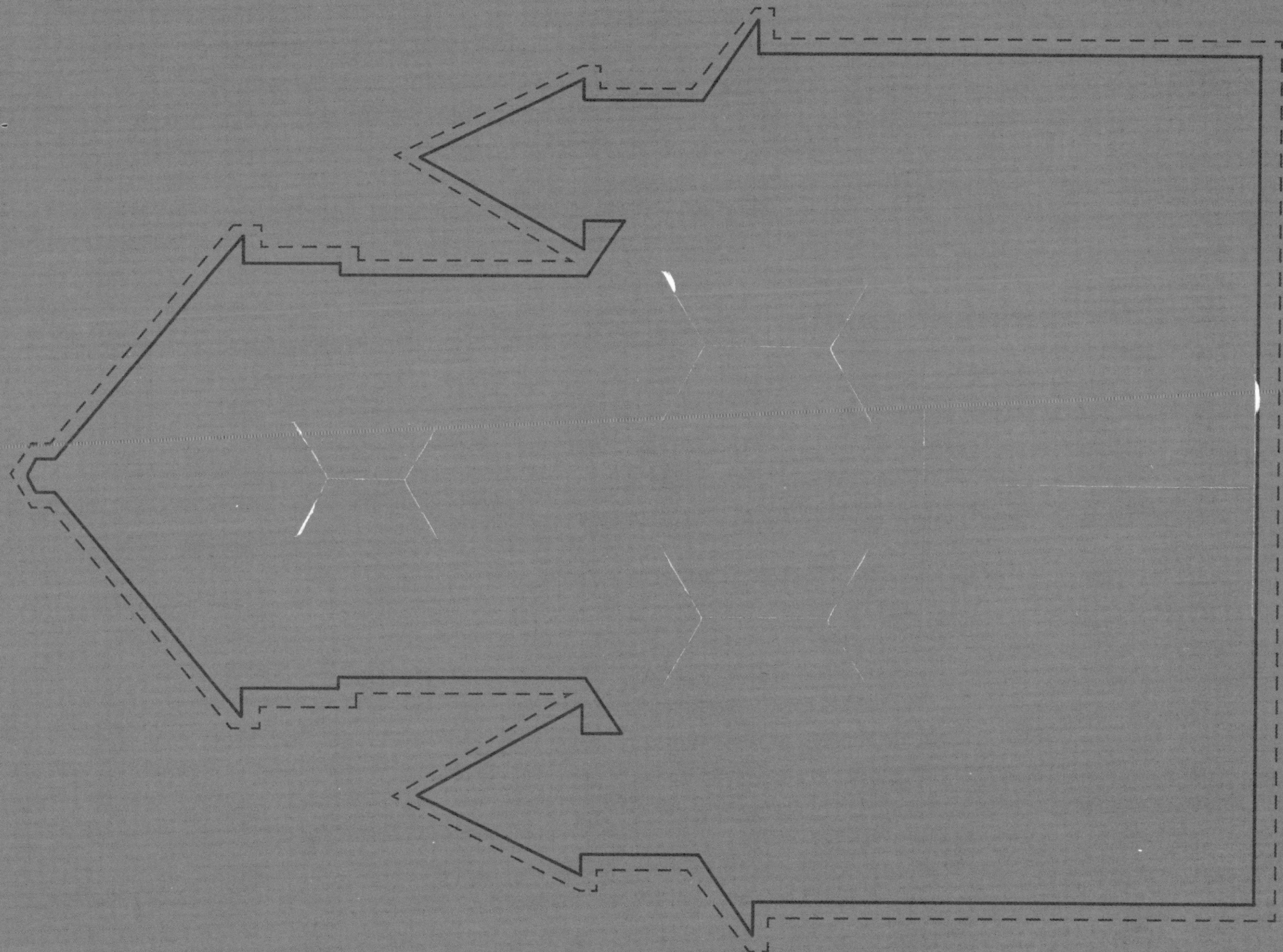

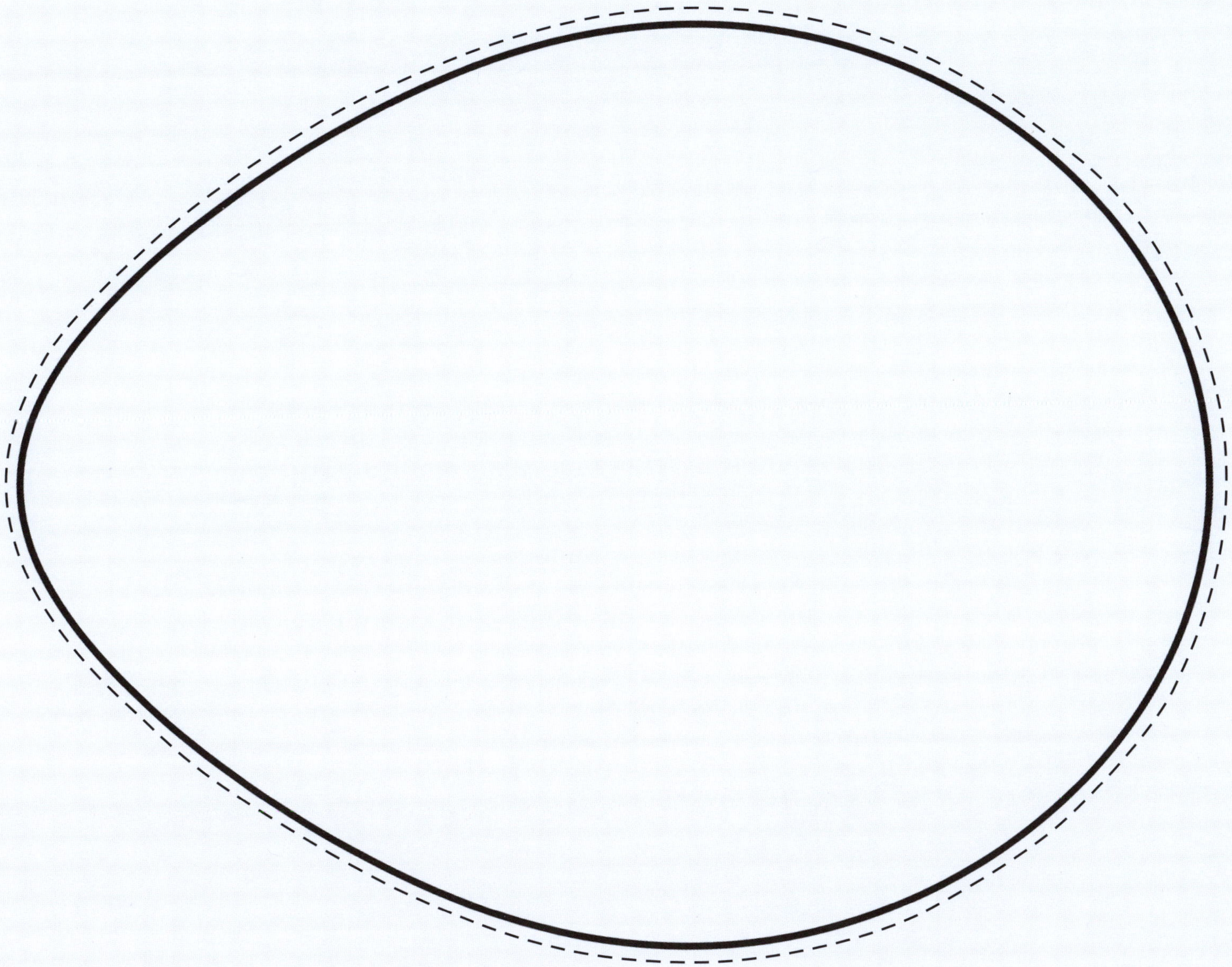